MARTYR MEETS WORLD

Abhijit Naskar is the twenty-first century Neuroscientist whose contributions in Cognitive and Behavioral Neuroscience have helped the world tackle the issues of mental illness, prejudice, hate, extremism, discrimination and segregation more effectively. As an untiring advocate of mental health and universal acceptance, he became a beloved best-selling author all over the world with his very first book "The Art of Neuroscience in Everything". With his pioneering ventures into the Neuropsychology of beliefs and biases, he has hugely contributed in the eradication of religious and cultural differences in our world, for which he is popularly hailed as the humanitarian scientist, who takes the human civilization in the path of sweet general harmony.

MARTYR

meets world

To Solve
The Hard Problem
of Inhumanity

ABHIJIT NASKAR

Martyr Meets World:

To Solve The Hard Problem of Inhumanity

Copyright © 2021 Abhijit Naskar

This is a work of non-fiction

An Amazon Publishing Company, 1st Edition, 2021

Printed in the United States of America

ISBN: 9798573968797

Also by Abhijit Naskar

The Art of Neuroscience in Everything
Your Own Neuron: A Tour of Your Psychic Brain
The God Parasite: Revelation of Neuroscience
The Spirituality Engine
Love Sutra: The Neuroscientific Manual of Love
Homo: A Brief History of Consciousness
Neurosutra: The Abhijit Naskar Collection
Autobiography of God: Biopsy of A Cognitive Reality
Biopsy of Religions: Neuroanalysis towards Universal
Tolerance
Prescription: Treating India's Soul
What is Mind?
In Search of Divinity: Journey to The Kingdom of Conscience
Love, God & Neurons: Memoir of a scientist who found
himself by getting lost
The Islamophobic Civilization: Voyage of Acceptance
Neurons of Jesus: Mind of A Teacher, Spouse & Thinker
Neurons, Oxygen & Nanak
The Education Decree
Principia Humanitas
The Krishna Cancer
Rowdy Buddha: The First Sapiens
We Are All Black: A Treatise on Racism
The Bengal Tigress: A Treatise on Gender Equality
Either Civilized or Phobic: A Treatise on Homosexuality
Wise Mating: A Treatise on Monogamy
Illusion of Religion: A Treatise on Religious
Fundamentalism
The Film Testament
Human Making is Our Mission: A Treatise on Parenting
I Am The Thread: My Mission
7 Billion Gods: Humans Above All
Lord is My Sheep: Gospel of Human
Morality Absolute
A Push in Perception
Let The Poor Be Your God
Conscience over Nonsense
Saint of The Sapiens
Time to Save Medicine
Fabric of Humanity

Build Bridges not Walls: In the name of Americana
The Constitution of The United Peoples of Earth
Lives to Serve Before I Sleep
When Humans Unite: Making A World Without Borders
All For Acceptance
Monk Meets World
Mission Reality
Citizens of Peace: Beyond The Savagery of Sovereignty
Operation Justice: To Make A Society That Needs No Law
See No Gender
The Gospel of Technology
Every Generation Needs Caretakers: The Gospel of
Patriotism
Aşkanjali: The Sufi Sermon
Mad About Humans: World Maker's Almanac
Revolution Indomable
When Call The People: My World My Responsibility
No Foreigner Only Family
Hurricane Humans: Give me accountability, I'll give you
peace
Ain't Enough to Look Human
Servitude is Sanctitude
Time To End Democracy: The Meritocratic Manifesto
I Vicdansaadet Speaking: No Rest Till The World is Lifted
Boldly Comes Justice: Sentient not Silent
Good Scientist: When Science and Service Combine
Sleepless for Society
Neden Türk: The Gospel of Secularism

DEDICATION

This book is dedicated to the humans, real ones.

CONTENTS

1. No Humanitarian
Only Human

ABHIJIT NASKAR

Genes don't carry dreams, not hereditarily that is, determination does. And as such, I have a dream - I have a dream of an akhand prithvi - of an undivided earth. But no dream can turn reality unless you are ready to die for it. I died long ago - I died as a person so I could live as an idea - as a dream – the dream behind my existence. You know why, because I was tired - I was tired of seeing narrowness and sectarianism creep into the veins of society and poison the sacred flow of life.

You know what a hero is - 9 out of 10 times it's someone who's too tired or too hungry or too cold to give a damn - I don't give a damn - I don't give a damn about the consequences, all I know is, the society that has been handed over to us by our ancestors can't possibly be a human society, it's a society of good-looking savages - and I won't sit still on my couch whining about it like a spineless bug either - it's my society, and I'll either turn it into a human one, or perish in the attempt.

I am no humanitarian, for the very term humanitarian is meaningless - I am just a plain, ordinary human - you are either a human or you are not - do you know what is a human - a human is one who cares for the welfare of others more than they care for the welfare of their own. Some may call it humanitarianism if they so desire, but it's just plain, ordinary humanity - that is, that's what humanity ought to be.

Right now all we have is sheer mockery of humanity, that's why we try to comfort ourselves with shallow notions of humanitarianism, charity and holiness. We want to believe in these theoretical concepts because it's far too easy to believe in a theoretical ideal than to take responsibility for the real deterioration of humanity in us. If you are human, you will be humanitarian - if you are human, you'll carry out charity - if you are human, you'll be holy - if you are human, you won't need all the pomp and ceremony of words to announce that you are acting as a real human being.

It's only the non-humans who need terms like humanitarianism, charity and holiness. Holy is not the one who constantly argues over the definition of holiness, holy is the one who quietly continues to help the people in need - the same holds true for charity, as well as for humanitarianism. To put it simply, there's no humanitarian, only human.

The day humankind becomes human, all humanitarian, charity and religious institutions will disappear from the face of earth. Humans awake with humanity see God in everyone, they don't need churches, temples and synagogues. Humans awake with humanity need no bible, quran or gita to tell right from wrong - they don't need humanitarian institutions to tackle crisis of human rights. They just stand up and act as human, and the whole planet is revolutionized.

2. The Question of Identity

ABHIJIT NASKAR

If your humanity is wide awake then just keep working as a human, away from the rotten show of words. Let people call you whatever they like, but don't ever make the mistake of sticking a label on your identity yourself, because the moment you do, is the moment you diminish the reach of your work. Let your work spread far and wide, penetrating into even the darkest and remotest corners of society.

Work with every community, belong to every community, but don't ever call only one community your own. Because this very act of exclusion negates the humanity in you - humanity that is beyond bounds - humanity that is beyond barriers - humanity that cannot be imprisoned by faith, facts of fame.

You are a human, that's all you need to know about your identity - know that you are human above all else, and all great things shall follow - you are the only impediment to your own fortune, you know why, because there is no such thing as fortune, whatever there is, it's all born out of human action - so if you can act out of an indomitable determination as a conscientious, courageous and compassionate human being, then there's nothing that you cannot achieve.

Achievement is 60 percent determination, 40 percent action. Notice that I give more importance to determination, than I do to action. That's because, sometimes you may require to take a little pause in absolute silence and immerse yourself in sheer contemplation, but never for a second you are to lose your determination, because the moment you do, is the moment you fail. Remember, failure is only a figment of your imagination, which cannot turn real till you give in to it.

But here's the trouble - sometimes that imagination feels so real due to the pressure of circumstances that the mind can't help but believe it to be the only reality in the world - what do we do then - work - that's the answer - work through everything - work till the goal is reached - you may feel devastated at times - that's perfectly alright - you are a human being of flesh and blood, not a machine - you ought to feel miserable at times - you ought to feel lonely at times - it takes a very selfish person to not feel lonely at times.

Better a trusting and caring human who feels all the emotions, good and bad, than a cold, calculating computer that feels nothing. If we are to progress as an advanced species, we'll do so by accepting our emotions, not leaving them behind. But mark you, accepting emotions doesn't mean letting them do whatever they want through you, accepting emotions means not resisting them, and from this acceptance rises the capacity to regulate those emotions - then you can choose whether or not to let those emotions be expressed through speech and behavior.

3.   Sonnet of Unity

Sonnet of Unity

I am vicdan,
I am saadet.
My life isn't mine,
It's your emanet.
Soy sanity,
Soy humanidad.
Life lies in service,
Selfishness kills vitalidad.
Ich bin inclusion,
Ich bin indivisible.
Mein kampf is unity,
Human and hate are incompatible.
Life divided brings degradation.
Growth comes through expansion.

(vicdan=conscience, saadet=joy, emanet=keepsake,
soy=I am, humanidad=humanity, vitalidad=vitality,
Ich bin=I am, mein kampf=my struggle)

16

4.   A Plain Act of Humanity

Anybody can draw courage from a hundred people, but when a hundred people draw courage from you, that's greatness - that's character - that's humanhood. This may be called humanitarianism by many, but the fact of the matter is, it's plain humanity. If you separate this act from everyday, ordinary living and place it in an exclusive club of so-called saintly souls, then you negate life itself – you negate the very fundamental of human life.

Human life has evolved from animal life, but there is a difference between human life and animal life. The fundamental drive behind animal life is personal survival, whereas the fundamental drive behind human life is collective welfare. The path of collective welfare is the path of humanity, all others are mere alleys of bestiality.

Remember, service alone is truth of the civilized society, all else is truth of the stone-age. Selfishness is savagery, service is humanity. Let me make it simpler still. Survival of the fittest is law of the jungle, sacrifice for the helpless is law of the human society. And anybody who realizes this simple principle in the very bones of their being, is the real human - that is the true humanitarian.

All humanitarians are reflections of me, I am the reflection of all humanitarians - all humans are reflections of me, I am the reflection of all humans. We all are reflections of each other, and as such we have as much capacity to change how the society behaves by behaving accountable ourselves regardless of society's approval, as the society has to drive our behaviors through conditioning.

Society is not the authority of your life, and you are not the authority of society either, you know why - you are the society, the society is you - so if you do something genuine, with or without the approval of society, sooner or later, that act becomes the act of society. At first they may disapprove and mock even, that's because originality scares the people of prejudice and ritual, but as you keep marching ahead with your head held high and chest emboldened in the path of your mission, your very determination mesmerizes the masses, and then they can't help but follow in your footsteps.

It's this simple, do what the society tells you and they would accept you as a member of society, but do what your mission tells you and they would place you on a pedestal as a torchbearer of society. But mark you, this has nothing to do with rebellion - let me elaborate - if you are thirsty and someone tells you water is bad for you, do you stop drinking water - and when you drink a glass of water to quench your thirst are you rebelling against the person - you are not - you are just doing what's natural - likewise, when you see the injustice and inequality in a society where indifference is accepted as the norm, standing up to eliminate such inhumanities is not an act of rebellion, it's an act of humanity - an act that is imperative if we are to turn our society actually civilized and human.

5.   When Calls A Revolution

To die for society is to live for eternity. Die for society, but not by obeying the filthy commands of society, instead die for society while trying to hold it up high from the darkness of rigidity and prejudice into the light of civilization and reason. But mark you, in this sacrifice for society, there's no place for recklessness. In fact, the act of lifting society calls for a limitless sense of accountability, without which it is very likely that you'd cause more harm than good.

Take the riot in Capitol for example. There is no place for weapons in civilized revolution (with the utter exception of war). Stand unbending against inhumanity, without weapons, without violence, only then will your revolution produce a better society. Only the savages speak the language of weapons, humans don't need weapons, their resolve is enough. Break, don't bend - that's the motto of civilized revolution.

When I say, your life has only one authority which is you, I am not talking about revolting against all sorts of authorities of society, even to the point of vandalizing sacred institutions, such as the Capitol. I don't respect the Capitol, because it is a place of authority, I respect it, because it represents the people of our nation. You cannot lift a people by recklessly disrespecting the institutions that represent the people. These institutions can turn corrupt from time to time surely, but eliminating that corruption requires thoughtful accountability, not mindless savagery.

The Capitol, for example, is not a building, it's a symbol of our democracy, and an assault on it is an assault on everything that we've achieved as a civilized people. Vandalizing a democratic institution is not civilized revolution, it is mob violence, at its worst. And revolution fueled by violence, doesn't solve anything - it only makes you feel good that you are finally getting your revenge.

You want revolution? Then dismantle all indifference and stand up - stand up and do not move - do not move from your conviction of justice - do not move from your conviction of equality - do not move from your conviction of humanity - do not move an inch - even if all the artilleries in the world are charged against you - do not move and do not harm - just stand - keep standing - keep standing like a pillar of insanity - an insanity for sanctity - an insanity for serenity - an insanity for unity - let them break every single bone in your body - let all the blood in your veins pour out - let every trace of life seep out of your wounds - but still do not move - till there is a single kernel of life left in you. This is what revolution looks like - this is what civilized revolution looks like - no guns, no bombs, not even a baton, just a whole lot of determination, that even the mighty gods cannot deter - a revolution that turns an animal world into a human world - a revolution that turns a jungle into a modern society – a revolution that turns distance into unity.

We cannot fight against brutes by becoming brutes ourselves. We must, not should, but must, be the epitome of the best of humankind, not the worst of it. Only when we act better than the brutes can we call ourselves human. Replying brutality with brutality only sustains the tradition of brutality - this tradition must be broken - and it can only be broken by heartlifting humans, not brainless brutes - it can only be broken by generation assimilation, not generation bigotry.

6. We Are Not Entitled to Comfort Yet

You know why brutality still exists in the world - it's because of the synthetic humans who stand still watching and do nothing. My concern is not that there's too much brutality in the world, my concern is that there's too many synthetic humans in the world who prefer indifference over humanity, for indifference is the worst form of inhumanity.

Take indifference to economic disparities for example. You know very well that, though you may have all the comfort and luxuries of modern living, there are people across the world who cannot even afford to have the very fundamentals of life. You may say, you've earned your comfort, so you are entitled to enjoy it - and it may be accepted to be true, if we were talking about self-obsessed apes - so long as you call yourself human, you are not entitled to any comfort whatsoever, as long as your very kind is suffering in some corner of the world - or even in your very neighborhood.

This is why, I don't like to treat myself with more than I need, because for every dollar spent on luxuries, someone somewhere goes hungry - and the only way to end this disparity is to contribute however we can to lift up those in distress - to improve their living - to make them self-reliant. If you can help even one person become self-reliant, it's the greatest achievement of social reform.

Young people often tell me, they want to do something for society, but they don't know where to begin - I tell them - gather some food and go out into the streets and into the remote villages to educate the ill-educated and the illiterate - first feed their stomach, then their soul - the purpose is not to make scholars out of them, but simply to open their eyes to the possibilities of the new world - the purpose is to help them become self-reliant.

And for whatever reason you think that your options are limited - remember, a mind that is determined for a purpose never runs out of options - it's not a matter of having options, it's a matter of making options out of sheer determination and persistence. Determination alone delivers destiny, for destiny is designed by those who are determined.

7.   Better Martyr than Maggot

While the meek population sits on their couch waiting for a miracle to happen, the determined designers of destiny stand up and make the miracle happen. A miracle is hundred percent persistence and zero percent miracle. In short, there is no miracle, only persistence.

Onward my would-be patriots - march ahead with an indefatigable zeal - freak not, flee not, keep walking and stop not till you reform at least a few lives around you. Remember, reforming society starts with reforming the lives of the people around you - and this very act is the solution to the hard problem of inhumanity. You don't have to revolutionize the whole world overnight, you just need to revolutionize one life with all the power in your veins. Why you ask - because a life lived only for the self is not human, but animal life.

We cannot rely on law enforcement to keep our world orderly forever - we cannot rely on soldiers to keep the world safe against acts of terror forever - or to put it more simply, we cannot let lives be lost fighting the troubles born of our own selfishness any longer. To those who like to call themselves human while taking pride in the death of soldiers I say - "grow up - stop taking pride in the death of soldiers - for once in your life act responsible and do something so that we no longer need the death of innocent soldiers to ensure peace on earth." We must work to reform the societal paradigm and establish conditions of health, education and serenity so that it no longer produces terrorists to spread terror.

Hence, let death come in its most vicious form - I as an accountable human accept it with utter grace - we the humans accept it with utter glory - for if we don't die, children cannot play in the park - if we do not die, lovers cannot walk freely hand in hand - if we do not die, the elderly cannot enjoy their favorite tv series over a cup of coffee. I have only one wish - when death comes, I want it to come in the shape of a bullet, not disease. But mark you, our first duty is not to die for nothing - but to live for the society - if we live and work for society, justice will live, inclusion will live, acceptance will live, peace will live - if we live and work for society, only then will the society live.

8.   If You Want Joy

It is a planet of people and it must be taken care of by the people - by each and every one of us. Remember, welfare of society hangs on a thin thread - the thread of individual accountability. Let others mock your involvement if they want. Those who have never woken up, what do they know about the concerns of the wakeful! Those who have never walked a mile, what do they know about the perils of the traveler!

If the society could, they would make selfish brutes out of every single person, and if they succeeded in doing so, then there wouldn't be any such thing as progress in our world, in fact, had they succeeded, we'd still be living in the jungle and in caves. We don't live in the jungle because some bravehearts just can't be tamed by the insecurity inducing warnings of society. Society advances on the shoulders of those who start walking most fervently without a single clue to the path.

If you have a purpose, the path manifests on its own. If you chase money, you'll be miserable your whole life and die as an insignificant name in the obituary list - if you chase name, sooner or later the money will come, but you'll still be miserable - but if you work for a purpose without thinking the least bit about money and name, then in time you'll have both the money and name, and more importantly joy will come chasing you along the way.

If you want joy, do one thing, burn to ashes in the flames of your purpose. If you want immortality, do one thing, burn to ashes in the flames of your purpose. Purpose is the path to peace. Purpose is the path to progress. Annihilate yourself for a purpose and you'll have all the joy in the world. Let others mock you as much as they want, you just keep on in your path.

But mark you, no matter what your purpose is, it must, one way or another, improve the lives of others around you - if not, then it's of no consequence. You may attain all the riches in the world, but if your achievements do not in some way help those in need, then what's the point of it all! It's a shallow achievement that brings prosperity only to you and does nothing to improve the lives of others.

9. No Such Thing as Humanitarian Crisis

We live in a society that teaches us to be concerned exclusively with the achievement of ourselves and to hell with the lives of others - our society teaches us to bow and lick the boots of billionaires while we behave like a filthy savage with the waitress or the construction worker or the janitor. I prefer to sit on the sidewalk and share a hotdog with a homeless person than sit at a fancy restaurant and have dinner with a billionaire.

The existence of billionaires is not a sign of prosperity, but a disgusting reminder of disparity. And society perpetuates this disparity by worshipping billionaires as deities. You see, the more you lack character, the more you worship fake glory. Those with character draw lessons from the life of everyone, without worshipping anyone. The characterless maggots worship billionaires as gods and aim to become billionaires themselves someday.

Let me put it simply - our purpose as civilized people must not be to become billionaires, but to end disparities, economic or otherwise. Disparities are not a humanitarian crisis, they are human crisis. In fact, there is no such thing as a humanitarian crisis, there's only human crisis. When you can realize this, you'll know that you've grown up from an animal into a human.

You see, every human is a humanitarian, but not all humanitarians are human. Why you ask? Because, not all humanitarians are genuinely concerned with the welfare of humanity, many of them make a show of being concerned only to attract attention - some even use humanitarianism as a cover for all sorts of monetary misdemeanor.

The sun gives light and warmth to the world, but it never says, 'call me this, call me that' - no, it just gives and gives and gives - it keeps giving without asking to be defined in particular terms - it doesn't even ask to be defined as the sun - it just keeps giving - such should be the act of a human - absolutely unselfish – absolutely uncorrupted - absolutely untainted by labels.

The sun doesn't care what you call it - I don't care what you call me - many people call me humanitarian, many call me humanist, many call me atheist, many call me socialist, many call me sufi, many call me radical - but all I know is that I am a human.

We may use words to define a human action, but we must never be stuck with words. Remember, words may try to explain an act, but to truly realize that act we must step beyond words. Realization begins where explanations end.

10. Two Types of Silence

Silence is the language of realization, action is the language of revolution. But what silence are we talking about here - for it may sound a bit vague - here, the silence is that of contemplation, through which tides of realization envelop your psychological universe - therefore, this silence is not to be taken as the silence of indifference.

You see, indifference is silent, so is realization, but the difference between the two is that the silence of indifference sustains a life of complacency, whereas the silence of realization pours in your veins such courage that you no longer are able to maintain indifference of any sort - wherever and whenever you see injustice and discrimination you leap in revolution - you leap with a strong conviction of equality and humaneness - you leap in an act of revolution.

But what exactly is revolution - does revolution mean simply mocking the bad - does revolution mean simply criticizing the corrupt - these may seem like an act of revolution, but they are not what revolution is all about. Let me elaborate.

Saying that all cops are corrupt, doesn't eliminate biases from law enforcement, just like saying all citizens are brainless morons doesn't make them accountable. Mocking people don't change anything, There's good and bad in every sector of society, and to lift the society we must empower the good while recognizing and eliminating the bad.

To help people recognize their prejudices and their biases, recognize and announce without shame your own prejudices and your own biases. Let me give you an example. Imagine you and me are having a conversation. Now - if I start by saying "you are an animal, admit it" - then I have already made myself distant from you - after I've called you an animal, no matter what I say, it's not going to contribute to a productive conversation, instead it'll be a debate in disguise. But if I start by saying "I am an animal, so are you - we all are - but we also have developed the brain capacity to be better than animals" - now it may invoke your curiosity to engage in the conversation.

And to engage most effectively ourselves in an actual fruitful dialogue - to engage in an act of eliminating inhumanities, such as systemic racism, from our society, we cannot speak as a democrat or republican - we cannot speak as a socialist or capitalist - we cannot speak as a believer or non-believer - we must speak as human beings.

You see - if we go back long enough, every single person on earth comes from a black mother. That makes all of us black, even if some look less black than others. Likewise, to eliminate homophobia, we cannot speak as straight or gay, we must speak as human beings - to eliminate sexism, we cannot speak as man, woman or anything else, we must speak as human beings.

11. The Law of Human Life

Our prime directive should be to build a world for the people, not for ideologies. Ideologies must serve people, instead of people serving ideologies. The world that we ought to raise is a world of the people, by the people, for the people. And for that - what the society needs is an MBA, that is Master of Benevolent Activism - what the society needs is an MD, that is Maverick of Determination - what the society needs is a PHD, that is Doctor of Perspiring Humanism.

It's time to be a hero, instead of holding out for one. The good people of history are all gone - MLK, Lincoln, Parks, Tolstoy, Teresa, Madiba and many more - all are gone, now it's time for us to be the new good people. We must be the new people - a new people with a new vision - a new people with a new perception - a new people with a rejuvenated and determined desire for equality, inclusion and assimilation - a new people bearing the torch of a new world, where religion is the people, philosophy is the people, salvation is the people.

Move mountains if mountains come in your way - shake heavens if heavens come in your way - destroy borders if borders come in your way -

drink entire rivers dry if rivers come in your way - but never - never ever let those impediments keep you from the path of a new world - from building a new society - a human society.

Pledge allegiance to no flag - pledge allegiance to no religion - pledge allegiance to no ideology - your concern is to be the people and people alone. But mark you, not pledging allegiance to any flag doesn't mean you are to disrespect the flag, because even if you do not hold any attachment to a certain flag, so long as a flag exists it represents a people.

I don't have any allegiance to any single flag, but still I cannot disrespect them either with words or with action, you know why, because a flag represents a people, therefore disrespecting a flag means disrespecting a people. Let me tell you a story. Once upon a time there was a great leader in one of the countries of planet earth. The military of a neighboring country had taken over a region there, but accompanied by his brave soldiers the great leader liberated that part of his country from oppression. In celebration when the people of his country laid down the flag of the oppressor for their leader to walk on, he refused - he refused to insult even the flag of an invading country, for such is the character of a true leader.

Leaders don't insult others to feel superior - they simply live as an epitome of courage, conscience and humility, and others can't help but follow on their own. It's a kind of magnetism that cannot be taught or learnt. It manifests on its own once you give your life to something greater than personal survival. Forget your need and do your deed - that's the law of human life - as opposed to, do the deed based on your personal need only, which is the law of animal life.

58

12. The Purifying Sonnet

The Purifying Sonnet

What the world needs is a helper,
Bold, brave and unbending.
What the world needs is a fire,
Daring, determined and unflinching.
What the world needs is a heartlifter,
Radical, revolutionary and rejuvenating.
What the world needs is a river,
Persistent, ceaseless and lifegiving.
What the world needs is a martyr,
Liberated, majestic and undying.
What the world needs is a flower,
Unconditioned, naïve and beautifying.
The world of today still lives in gutter.
It is our duty to be the purifier.

13. Motive Makes The Difference

64

Little things that sustain your soul are okay, but remember, once you start indulging in self-gratification with no moderation whatsoever, you start sail on a slippery course of degradation. Luxury is the enemy of growth. Growth is the shy kid in the block - the moment it's around riches, it raises a wall and hides away in some dark corner of your mind never to come up to the surface. However, the more you surround it with humility, growth flourishes like nothing you've ever seen.

So, be humble, be simple and focus on your work, not on your appearance. Focus on character, not clothes. If even half the people of earth paid more attention to character than clothes, justice and equality will envelop the world sooner than you can imagine. Character is more precious than suits, mansions and cars. We all will soon disappear but our character will live on.

Also, in the course of lifting the society some may come along and say that you are full of yourself - but don't lose heart at their mockery, for the difference between humanitarianism and narcissism is in intention. You cannot breathe life into a dead society without being absurdly confident of your conviction, which may appear to some as narcissism. The narcissist is sure of their conviction because it makes them feel good about themselves - the humanitarian is sure of their conviction because it makes them sacrifice all for the good of society.

You see - the terrorist is a radical, so is the reformer. The difference is in their motive - the terrorist wants to build an exclusive society, whereas the reformer wants to build an inclusive society. In short, the terrorist takes the society backward, the reformer takes it forward – and the way forward is the way of inclusion – the way of celebrating diversity.

To recognize diversity is science, to celebrate it is humanity. Nothing is absolute in our world. Everything is ever-evolving, everything is every-changing, and our purpose as a sentient, ever-evolving species is to elevate our minds from the illusion of separation towards the truth of unity. Once we achieve that goal, that one, absolute, unified existence - progress will become mere child's play to us.

Right now most of our energy is spent on dealing with the troubles caused by separation, by duality - once we have resolved that, that is, once we have become an actual united and civilized species, then my friend we can start working on the real problems of our world, such as poverty, homelessness, human trafficking, climate change, terrorism and many more.

March forward penetrating the gloom of ritual and rigidity, and the path will reveal itself. The universe reveals its secrets to the brave and the daring not to the bigoted and the rigid. The problem is, revenue has become the grand aim of our civilization - but this can't be - we can't allow it to be. Why you ask? Because a species chasing revenue creates more and more economic disparities which leads to a variety of other societal disparities, but a species in the course of improving human condition, not only improves human condition but also generates revenue in the process.

Where we place our attention makes a great deal of difference in terms of health, sanity and serenity for our whole humankind in the long run. Without the concern for social welfare, economic growth is inhumanly proportional to economic disparity.

We are nothing without our society, so if our achievements do not improve our society, they are all meaningless. The individual life is meaningful only when it leaves a mark on the lives of others. A candle is useless if it stays unburnt - its purpose is fulfilled when it burns itself while giving light to others.

14. To End Persecution
Once and For All

We are all living in a virtual reality constructed by our brain - the least we can do as a civilized species - as thinking and feeling human beings - is live in a reality of our own choosing instead of one imposed on us by our selfish survival instincts. We have the brain capacity to do so - the question is, will we!

Take religious authoritarianism for example. When we submit to the authority of a religious institution we feel secure and comfortable, because we wash our hands of all moral responsibilities towards our own life as well as that of our society - and in doing so we keep quiet while the religious authorities continue to commit acts of homophobia, misogyny, sexism, bigotry, segregation and sectarianism. Our silence turns into the fuel for religious disharmony and terrorism – thus we contribute to the making of a reality full with hate and prejudice.

The point is, if we do not stand up to religious authoritarianism, religious harmony will remain fiction forever. In fact, if we do not stand up to sectarianism, prejudice and bigotry, no matter their background, future generations will continue to face persecution, one way or another.

We are not going to have harmony and inclusion in our world by sitting quietly on our couch and letting the institutions do whatever they want. Each of us must stand up against rigidity, prejudice and sectarianism no matter where we are and no matter what we do for living. To create an inclusive society is as much a responsibility of a construction worker, as it is of a scientist - it is as much a responsibility of a waitress, as it is of a politician - it is as much a responsibility of a janitor, as it is of a theologian.

Profession or status doesn't make us high or low in worth, our sense of responsibility towards society does. To feel no responsibility towards society is the greatest sin of civilization. There is no sin greater than indifference, no blasphemy greater than bigotry, no sacrilege greater than segregation.

Some may argue, just for the sake of argument that how can indifference be worse than say homicide! I say, it's worse because in homicide the atrocity is obvious, whereas in indifference it is not so - in fact, in indifference unless we look closely we may not even notice any atrocity. But here's the thing - staying silent in the face of an atrocity is worse than that atrocity itself, because you are inadvertently facilitating that atrocity without taking the blame for it. In short, indifference is acceptable from a vegetable, not from a human being.

15. Divinity for Sale
(The Sonnet)

Divinity for Sale
(The Sonnet)

When a book becomes religion,
And doctrines become divinity,
Holiness remains speculation,
Society loses sight of humanity.
When institutions claim authority,
And sleeping masses comply,
Religion disappears altogether,
What remains is potential gone awry.
When popes and pundits sell faith,
In the name of divine supremacy,
Rigidity overrules common sense,
And reason is hailed as blasphemy.
But there is a cure for all this atrocity.
It is called individual curiosity.

16. Weakness is Growth

80

No paradigm is perfect - no structure is perfect - no system is perfect - no matter how carefully we construct it, it will never be at its absolute best without flaws, without prejudice, without biases - but the human society is not going to be advanced enough for a long, long time to live without paradigm, so what is the way out - there is only one way - to admit that our paradigm is not perfect and then hand it over to the future generation with a little reminder that every paradigm must be made anew by the new generation based on their time and age. So we tell them - take this paradigm which we built for ourselves, but don't obey it as gospel, instead accept the elements that apply to your time and make them evolve - make them evolve according to the needs of your time - think of new elements if necessary - reform the paradigm however you see fit - and never be afraid to evolve - dare to reform your society with the fresh whiff of thought and conscience - only then can we continue to progress as civilized humankind with less and less chaos caused by rigidity, extremism and bigotry.

We must set an example as a wise and humble people for the future generation, only then will they be able to eliminate war and conflicts from this planet once and for all. And the best way to do so is to start by admitting our shortfalls and our ineptitude. We must stay as far away as possible from pretending to be perfect and flawless people. Pretend perfection does more harm to the society than imperfection. In fact, imperfection is part of life and often they add variation to life, but by pretending to be without imperfection one starts walking on a path of decay.

Think of disease for example. We all know when we are sick, we acknowledge the disease then we take medicine to treat that disease. Likewise, what's wrong with having shortfalls - what's wrong with having weaknesses - accept those shortfalls and those weaknesses and treat them with conscience - only then can there be progress - only then can there be ascension, both for the self as well as society.

Rigidity to admit no wrong can come in all shapes and sizes - sometimes it comes in the shape of religious fundamentalism, and other times it comes in the shape of intellectual fundamentalism. Arrogance of intellect turns a person so blind that in an attempt to sound profound and logical they lose all touch with reality as well as humanity, just like religious fundamentalists do in their attempt to sound spiritually superior.

Let me tell you this - I'd rather sit amongst illiterate villagers and actually talk about life, than sit amidst a bunch of intellectual morons and pretend to talk about life. A life of arrogance, be it religious arrogance or intellectual arrogance, is anything but human life - for a life of arrogance is a life devoid of conscience and a life devoid of conscience is death in disguise.

Think of conscience, dream of conscience, live of conscience - think of courage, dream of courage, live of courage - think of character, dream of character, live of character. Remember, every weakness is growth in disguise. You say "show me the path out of weakness", I say, "weakness is the path, walk on it daringly and it'll turn into strength". The tragedy of life is that, all know weakness, very few know strength - all know rigidity, very few know sanity - all know death, very few know life.

17. When You Are Accountable

Die to death and you'll wake up to life - die to death, you'll wake up to strength - die to death, you'll wake up to conscience - those who want to continue sleeping, let them sleep - but you must wake yourself up. People die more in fear of death than death itself. When death comes nothing can save you, but till then, nothing can kill you. So why waste your precious potential on useless worry!

Throw all worry overboard and leap into life - leap into life and achieve the unachievable - leap into life and accomplish the unthinkable - leap into life and realize the impossible. Person lives only once, live so big that your very existence turns into a definition of life. But mark you, to live big doesn't mean to live in luxury, it means to live for a cause - for a purpose. You should live because you have a purpose, not because it's not your time to die yet.

At the same time you must remember, if your purpose only serves your own benefit, then it is no human purpose, but only a primitive chase. Human purpose involves the benefit of not just the individual but also the collective. Without a sense of communion with the collective, all of human civilization will collapse to dust.

Civilization starts with accountability. And only with accountability we'll initiate real democracy in our society - only with accountability we'll initiate real inclusion in our society - only with accountability we'll initiate upliftment in our society. When you are accountable, nobody can stop you from speaking up - when you are accountable nobody can stop you from listening - when you are accountable nobody can stop you from rise against the wide-spread pandemic of indifference. Mark you, indifference is far more dangerous than a viral outbreak. And this indifference has such a grip over people that neither reason nor sentiment can penetrate their thick skull to make them distinguish humanity from inhumanity.

A population living with indifference remains oblivious to the inhumanities of society. And as such they shut their eyes, ears and mouth to the harms around them and when they do open them, they do so to defend their so-called integrity, not to speak up against inhumanity. And the point is, there is no magical wand with the touch of which you can suddenly turn these sick, spineless insects into thinking and feeling human beings. The best you can do is to be the example of humanity with your bold, brave and conscientious acts of humaneness, inclusion and accountability. Let sleeping bugs sleep - you are a human, you do not have the primitive luxury to keep sleeping while your society suffers. Only dogs and donkeys sleep while their society suffers, not humans.

18. Not One But Two Democracies

Dialogue is the road to democracy, a functional democracy that is. And democracy is the road to everything that is civilized in our society. Democracy is not the destination, it is the path. It is with which we move ahead towards goals of grand significance. But first we must question what is democracy? There is not one but two democracies - one that is a form of government, and another which is the very foundation of a civilized society.

Democracy as a form of government is only the most primitive form of democracy. The democracy that we ought to be concerned with is the democracy which is the foundation of civilized society. So, what is this second democracy? Democracy as a foundation of civilized society is simply an uncorrupted and bold sense of inclusion and equality – a democracy where people come first, then everything else. It has nothing to do with politicians - it has nothing to do with bureaucrats - it has nothing to do with law enforcement - for democracy is the blood of a civilized society - as such it is to flow in the veins of every single creature called human.

If you are really a human, you are democratic, that is there is no place for sectarianism in your heart whatsoever. It is as simple as this - democracy means non-sectarianism - democracy means non-partisanism - democracy means non-racism. In short, democracy is another name for unity. Hence, a democratic species means a united species. And an undemocratic species is no human species. A species indivisible, that's what democracy looks like. The shape of democracy is defined by our sense of unity, not by our ideological loyalty, not by our nationalist stubbornness, not by our religious rigidity.

Our rigidity not only divides us from society, it also diminishes our humanity. In short, rigidity keeps an animal from becoming a human. Take religious rigidity for example. In an attempt to record the thoughts of Christ and secure a place of authority for him in the society, early followers of Christ turned him into a book - they called it Bible. Then later disciples began to worship the bible as the religion called Christianity. In their eyes the book became religion, and in the process they lost sight of the very inclusive spirit of Christ. As a result, all that remained was authoritarianism, but no religion. It is this simple, where there is authoritarianism there cannot be religion, where there is religion there cannot be authoritarianism.

Religion is not a book - religion is people, religion is life - and how can you bind life in a book. Love and inclusion know no books, they reside in the heart of every human being on earth. You know why - because books only talk about love, but it's the heart where love is born. Once you recognize this principle in the very core of your existence, every civilized concept will begin to appear as what they are - manifestations of love - democracy will reveal itself as love - secularism will reveal itself as love - humanism will reveal itself as love - in this love you'll find sanity - in this love you'll find sanctity - in this love you'll find humanity.

19. Shalom Civilization
(The Sonnet)

Shalom Civilization
(The Sonnet)

Without accountability there's no civilization,
For it is the line between human and animal.
Without integrity there's no civilization,
For it is the line between human and vegetable.
Without sanctity there's no civilization,
For it is the line between sanity and savagery.
Without amity there's no civilization,
For it is the line between humanity and machinery.
Without conscience there's no civilization,
For it is the line between order and upheaval.
Without character there's no civilization,
For it is the line between life and survival.
Civilization is a small word with a universe inside.
To unfold it requires a species without divide.

20. I Am Civilization

We ourselves are the instrument of humanity and inhumanity, whichever you choose to nourish will manifest through your behavior - and your behavior is the gateway to a civilized society. Only accountability will rescue humans from their own inhumanity - accountability that begins not with an ideology, or with a party, or with a religion - accountability that begins with the individual. Conquer your own inhumanity and inhumanity of this world will start to fade away.

Remember, if you do not find civilization inside you, you'll never find it outside. You can walk to the ends of the earth in search of civilization, but you'll only find yourself. Call upon the civilization that lies dormant within you - call it up with all your might and watch it spread its magnificent majesty through your veins and your nerves.

We spent ages trying to come out of our cradle in Africa only to imprison ourselves in our insane pursuit of productivity. In the early days nature made us pursue survival like crazy, today society makes us pursue productivity like crazy. Neither of these two is a sign of advancement - we have merely exchanged one insanity for another. Yet this insanity of productivity is considered absolute sanity - in fact, it is considered to be the foundation stone of our society. This can't be - this can't continue, because if we let this continue, then soon we'll have all the productivity in the world but that productivity will not have a single trace of life and love in it. Is this what we want - I don't - do you?

If you don't, then the answer is only one - be what you want your society to be. If you want civilization, be the epitome of civilization - if you want democracy, be the epitome of democracy - if you want humanity, be the epitome of humanity. Go on saying - "I am civilization, I am democracy, I am humanity". The revolutionary is the revolution - the reformer is the reformation.

You are never too old to reform your society. Expand yourself, risk everything for civilization and ask nothing in return, and all reform will follow. Come, be bold, be the cause of civilization. And remember, if you try to rule people, you'll end up a slave to your arrogance, but if you try to serve them, you'll become the ruler of the whole world.

Keep working ceaselessly to raise a civilization. Say to yourself, "I have no path, for I am the path." You are the path, you are the journey, you are the destination - you are all in one. Once you realize this, what power does the society have over you to keep you from achieving your dreams, no matter how absurd or utopian they appear to the sleeping masses!

The fabric of progress unfolds on the odyssey of impossible dreams. Dream my friend - dream without fear - dream without limits - dream without the influence of society's conditions - dream beyond the very duality of possible and impossible - engulf your whole being with your dream, then with that dream engulf the whole world. One dream can deliver our planet from darkness to dawn, the question is, can you persevere past your breaking point for that dream!

BIBLIOGRAPHY

Archer M., (2000), Being Human: The Problem of Agency. Cambridge University Press.

Archer M., (2003), Structure, Agency and the Internal Conversation. Cambridge University Press.

Adolphs R (2003) Cognitive neuroscience of human social behaviour. Nature Rev Neurosci 4: 165–178.

Adolphs R, Tranel D, Damasio AR (2003) Dissociable neural systems for recognizing emotions. Brain Cogn 52: 61–69.

Afton, A. D. (1985). Forced copulation as a reproductive strategy of male lesser scaup: A field test of some predictions. - Behaviour 92, p. 146-167.

Allison T, Puce A, McCarthy G. (2000) Social perception from visual cues: role of the STS region. Trends Cogn Sci 4: 267–278.

Andresen, Jensine, and Robert Forman, eds. Cognitive Models and Spiritual Maps. Bowling Green, Ohio: Imprint Academic, 2000.

Ashbrook, James, and Carol Albright. The Humanizing Brain: Where Religion and Neuroscience Meet. Cleveland, OH: Pilgrim Press, 1997.

Azari, Nina, Janpeter Nickel, Gilbert Wunderlich, Michael Niedeggen, Harald Hefter, Lutz Tellmann, Hans Herzog, Petra Stoerig, Dieter Birnbacher, and Rudiger Seitz. "Neural Correlates of Religious Experience." European Journal of Neuroscience 13, no. 8 (2001)

Agar, N. (2004). Liberal eugenics: In defence of human enhancement. London: Blackwell Publishing.

Alteheld, N., Roessler, G., Vobig, M., & Walter, R. (2004). The retina implant new approach to a visual prosthesis. Biomedizinische Technik, 49(4), 99–103.

Antal, A., Nitsche, M. A., Kincses, T. Z., Kruse, W., Hoffmann, K. P., & Paulus, W. (2004a). Facilitation of visuo-motor learning by transcranial direct current stimulation of the motor and extrastriate visual areas in humans. European Journal of Neuroscience, 19(10), 2888–2892.

Bhat Z, Kumar, S, Bhat H (2015) In vitro meat production. Challenges and benefits over conventional meat production. J Sci Food Agric 14: 241–248

Bernstein R. J., (1967), John Dewey. New York: Washington Square Press.

Bernstein R.J., (1971), Praxis and Action: Contemporary Philosophies of Human Activity. Philadelphia: University of Pennsylvania Press.

Bernstein R.J., (1976), The Restructuring Social and Political Thought.

Bernstein R.J., (1983), Beyond Relativism and Objectivism: Science, Hermeneutics, and Praxis. Philadelphia: University of Pennsylvania Press.

Bernstein R.J., (1986), Philosophical Profiles. Philadelphia: University of Pennsylvania Press.

Bernstein R.J., (1991), New Constellation. Cambridge: MIT Press.

Barash, D. P. (1977). Sociobiology of rape in mallards (Anas platyrhynchos): Responses of the mated male. - Science 197, p. 788-789.

Berger, J. (1986). Wild horses of the great basin: Social competition and population size. - The University of Chicago Press, Chicago.

Birkhead, T. R., Johnson, S. D. & Nettleship, D. N. (1985). Extra-pair matings and mate guarding in the common murre Uria aalge. - Anim. Behav. 33, p. 608-619.

Beauregard, Mario, and Vincent Paquette. "Neural Correlates of a Mystical Experience in Carmelite Nuns." Neuroscience Letters 405, no. 3 (2006)

Benson, Herbert. Timeless Healing: The Power and Biology of Belief. New York: Scribner, 1996

Bogen, J.E.(1995a), 'On the neurophysiology of consciousness: Part I. An overview', Consciousness and Cognition, 4.

Bogen, J.E. (1995b), 'On the neurophysiology of consciousness: Part II. Constraining the semantic problem', Consciousness and Cognition, 4.

Bremner, J. D., R. Soufer, et al. (2001). "Gender differences in cognitive and neural correlates of remembrance of emotional words." Psychopharmacol Bull 35 (3).

Brothers, L. (2002). The social brain: A project for integrating primate behavior and neurophysiology in a new domain. In J. T. Cacioppo et al. (Eds.), Foundations in neuroscience. Cambridge, MA: MIT Press.

Buss, D. D. (2003). Evolutionary Psychology: The New Science of Mind, 2nd ed. New York: Allyn & Bacon.

Buss, D. M. (1989). "Conflict between the sexes: Strategic interference and the evocation of anger and upset." J Pers Soc Psychol 56 (5).

Buss, D. M. (1995). "Psychological sex differences. Origins through sexual selection." Am Psychol 50 (3).

Buss, D. M. (2002). "Review: Human Mate Guarding." Neuro Endocrinol Lett 23 (Suppl 4).

Buss, D. M., and D. P. Schmitt (1993). "Sexual strategies theory: An evolutionary perspective on human mating." Psychol Rev 100 (2).

Blakemore SJ, Decety J (2001) From the perception of action to the understanding of intention. Nature Rev Neurosci 2: 561.

Bruce C, Desimone R, Gross CG (1981) Visual properties of neurons in a polysensory area in superior temporal sulcus of the macaque. J Neurophysiol 46: 369–384.

Buccino G, Vogt S, Ritzl A, Fink GR, Zilles K, Freund HJ, Rizzolatti G (2004) Neural circuits underlying imitation of hand actions: an event related fMRI study. Neuron 42: 323–34.

Colapietro V., (1988), "Human Agency: The Habits of Our Being."

Southern Journal of Philosophy, XXVI, 2, pp. 153-68.

Colapietro V., (1992), "Purpose, Power, and Agency." The Monist, 75, 4 (October) pp. 423-44.

Colapietro V., (2003), "Signs and their vicissitudes: Meanings in excess of consciousness and functionality." Logica, Dialogica, Ideologica, a cure di Susan Petrilli e Patrizia Calefato (Milano: Mimesis), pp. 221-36.

Colapietro V., (2004a), "C. S. Peirce's Reclamation of Teleology." Nature in American Philosophy, ed. Jean De Groot (Washington, D.C.: Catholic University Press of America), pp. 88-108.

Colapietro V., (2004b), "Portrait of a Historicist: An Alternative Reading of Peircean Semiotic." Semiotiche, 2/04 [maggio 2004], pp. 49-68.

Colapietro V., (2006), "Engaged Pluralism: Between Alterity and

Sociality." The Pragmatic Century: Conversations with Richard J. Bernstein (Albany, NY: SUNY Press), pp. 39-68.

Colapietro V., (2009), "Habit, Competence, and Purpose." Forthcoming in The Transactions of the Charles S. Peirce Society. Calder AJ, Keane J, Manes F, Antoun N, Young AW (2000) Impaired recognition and experience of disgust following brain injury. Nature Neurosci 3: 1077–1078.

Carey DP, Perrett DI, Oram MW (1997) Recognizing, understanding and reproducing actions. In: Jeannerod M, Grafman J (eds) Handbook of neuropsychology. Vol. 11: Action and cognition. Elsevier, Amsterdam.

Carr L, Iacoboni M, Dubeau MC, Mazziotta JC, Lenzi GL (2003) Neural mechanisms of empathy in humans: a relay from neural systems for imitation to limbic areas. Proc Natl Acad Sci USA 100: 5497–5502.

Changeux JP, Ricoeur P (1998) La nature et la règle. Odile Jacob, Paris.

Cochin S, Barthelemy C, Roux S, Martineau J (1999) Observation and execution of movement: similarities demonstrated by quantified electroencephalograpy. Eur J Neurosci 11: 1839– 1842.

Chomsky Noam, (2017) Requiem for the American Dream

Chomsky Noam, (2016) Who Rules the World?

Chomsky Noam, (2010) How the World Works

Churchland, P.S. (1986), Neurophilosophy (Cambridge, MA: The MIT Press).

Churchland, P.S. & Ramachandran, V.S. (1993), 'Filling in: Why Dennett is wrong', in Dennett and His Critics:

Demystifying Mind, ed. B. Dahlbom (Oxford: Blackwell Scientific Press).

Churchland, P.S., Ramachandran, V.S. & Sejnowski, T.J. (1994), 'A critique of pure vision', in Large- scale Neuronal Theories of the Brain, ed. C. Koch & J.L. Davis (Cambridge, MA: The MIT Press).

Crick, F. (1994), The Astonishing Hypothesis: The Scientific Search for the Soul (New York: Simon and Schuster).

Crick, F. (1996), 'Visual perception: rivalry and consciousness', Nature, 379.

Crick, F. & Koch, C. (1992), 'The problem of consciousness', Scientific American, 267.

Craig AD (2002) How do you feel? Interoception: the sense of the physiological condition of the body. Nature Rev Neurosci 3: 655–666.

Damasio, A (2003a) Looking for Spinoza. Harcourt Inc. Damasio A (2003b) Feeling of emotion and the self. Ann NY Acad Sci 1001: 253–261.

d'Aquili, Eugene. "Senses of Reality in Science and Religion." Zygon 17, no 4 (1982)

d'Aquili, Eugene. "The Biopsychological Determinants of Religious Ritual Behavior." Zygon 10, no. 1 (1975)

d'Aquili, Eugene. "The Myth-Ritual Complex: A Biogenetic Structural Analysis." Zygon 18, no. 3 (1983)

d'Aquili, Eugene, and Andrew Newberg. The Mystical Mind: Probing the Biology of Religious Experience. Minneapolis: Fortress Press, 1999.

Daly DD. 1958. Ictal affect. Am J Psychiatry.

Damasio, A. (1994) Descartes' Error: Emotion, Reason and the Human Brain. New York, Putnams.

Damasio, A. (1999) The Feeling of What Happens: Body, Emotion and the Making of Consciousness. London, Heinemann.

Darwin, C. (1859) On the Origin of Species by Means of Natural Selection. London, Murray.

Darwin, C. (1871) The Descent of Man and Selection in Relation to Sex. London, John Murray.

Darwin, C. (1872) The Expression of the Emotions in Man and Animals. London, John Murray; also published 1965, Chicago, University of Chicago Press.

Dawkins, M.S. (1987) Minding and mattering. In C. Blakemore and S. Greenfield (eds) Mindwaves. Oxford, Blackwell, 151-60.

Dawkins, R. (1976) The Selfish Gene. Oxford, Oxford University Press; a new edition, with additional material, was published in 1989.

Dawkins, R. (1986) The Blind Watchmaker. London, Longman.

Di Pellegrino G, Fadiga L, Fogassi L, Gallese V, Rizzolatti G (1992) Understanding motor events: A neurophysiological study. Exp Brain Res 91: 176–80.

Deikman, A.J. (2000) A functional approach to mysticism. Journal of Consciousness Studies 7(11-12), 75-91.

Delmonte, M.M. (1987) Personality and meditation. In M. West (ed.) The Psychology of Meditation. Oxford, Clarendon Press, 118-32.

Dennett, D.C. (1987) The Intentional Stance. Cambridge, MA, MIT Press.

Dennett, D.C. (1988) Quining qualia. In A.J. Marcel and E. Bisiach (eds)

Consciousness in Contemporary Science. Oxford, Oxford University Press, 42-77.

Dennett, D.C. (1991) Consciousness Explained. Boston, MA, and London, Little, Brown and Co.

Dennett, D.C. (1995a) Darwin's Dangerous Idea. London, Penguin.

Dennett, D.C. (1995b) The unimagined preposterousness of zombies. Journal of Consciousness Studies 2(4), 322-6.

Dennett, D.C. (1995c) Cog: steps towards consciousness in robots. In T. Metzinger (ed.) Conscious Experience. Thorverton, Devon, Imprint Academic, 471-87.

Dennett, D.C. (1995d) The path not taken. Behavioral and Brain Sciences 18, 252-3; commentary on N. Block, On a confusion about a function of consciousness. Behavioral and Brain Sciences 18, 227.

Dennett, D.C. (1996a) Facing backwards on the problem of consciousness. Journal of Consciousness Studies 3(1), 4-6.

Dennett, D.C. (1996b) Kinds of Minds: Towards an Understanding of Consciousness. London, Weidenfeld & Nicolson.

Dennett, D.C. (1997) An exchange with Daniel Dennett. In J. Searle (ed.) The Mystery of Consciousness. New York, New York Review of Books, 115-19.

Dennett, D.C. (1998) The myth of double transduction. In S.R. Hameroff, A.W. Kaszniak and A. C. Scott (eds) Toward a Science of Consciousness: The Second Tucson Discussions and Debates. Cambridge, MA, MIT Press, 97-107.

Dennett, D.C. (1998b) Brainchildren: Essays on Designing Minds. Cambridge, MA, MIT Press.

Dennett, D.C. (2001) The fantasy of first person science. Debate with D. Chalmers, Northwestern University, Evanston, IL, February 2001.

Dennett, D.C. (2003) Freedom Evolves. New York, Penguin.

Dennett, D.C. and Kinsbourne, M. (1992) Time and the observer: the where and when of consciousness in the brain. Behavioral and Brain Sciences 15, 183-247, including commentaries and authors' responses.

Dewey J., (1911 [1977]), "Epistemological Realism: The Alleged Ubiquity of the Knowledge Relation." Journal of Philosophy, VIII, 20 (September 28, 1911).

Dewhurst, Kenneth, and A. W. Beard. "Sudden Religious Conversions in Temporal Lobe Epilepsy." British Journal of Psychiatry 117 (1970)

Dewhurst K, Beard AW. Sudden religious conversions in temporal lobe epilepsy. 1970 Epilepsy Behav 2003

Devinsky O, Lai G. Spirituality and religion in epilepsy. Epilepsy Behav 2008.

Devinsky, O., Morrell, MJ, Vogt, BA. (1995) 'Contribution of anterior cingulate cortex to behavior', Brain, 118.

Douglas Stone A., Chapter 24, The Indian Comet, in the book Einstein and the Quantum, Princeton University Press, Princeton, New Jersey, 2013.

E. Horvitz, "One Hundred Year Study on Artificial Intelligence: Reflections and Framing," ed: Stanford University, 2014.

Einstein A. (1925). "Quantentheorie des einatomigen idealen Gases". Sitzungsberichte der Preussischen Akademie der Wissenschaften.

Eckhart Meister, Selected Writings

Egidi R., ed. (1999), "Von Wright and 'Dante's Dream': Stages in a Philosophical Pilgrim's Progress", in In Search of a New Humanism: the Philosophy of G.H. von Wright, ed. by R. Egidi, Kluwer, Dordrecht.

Fadiga L, Fogassi L, Pavesi G, Rizzolatti G (1995) Motor facilitation during action observation: a magnetic stimulation study. J Neurophysiol 73: 2608–2611.

Fogassi L, Gallese V, Fadiga L, Rizzolatti G (1998) Neurons responding to the sight of goal directed hand/arm actions in the parietal area PF (7b) of the macaque monkey. Soc Neurosci Abs 24:257.5.

Frith U, Frith CD (2003) Development and neurophysiology of mentalizing. Philos Trans R Soc Lond B Biol Sci 358: 459.

Farah, M.J. (1989), 'The neural basis of mental imagery', Trends in Neurosciences, 10.

Finlay BL, Darlington RB (1995) Linked regularities in the development and evolution of mammalian brains. Science 268.

Freud, S. "The Interpretation of Dreams", 1900

Freud, S. "Selected papers on hysteria and other psychoneuroses" Journal of Nervous and Mental Disease 1909.

Freud, S. "The Origin and Development of Psychoanalysis", 1910

Freud, S. "Psychopathology of everyday life", 1914

Freud, S. "Beyond the Pleasure Principle", 1920

Frith, C.D. & Dolan, R.J. (1997), 'Abnormal beliefs: Delusions and memory', Paper presented at the May,

1997, Harvard Conference on Memory and Belief.

Gay, Volney, ed. Neuroscience and Religion. Plymouth, UK: Lexington Books, 2009.

Gazzaniga, M. S. (1985). The social brain. New York: Basic Books.

Gazzaniga, M.S. (1993), 'Brain mechanisms and conscious experience', Ciba Foundation Symposium, 174.

Geschwind N. "Behavioural changes in temporal lobe epilepsy". Psychol Med. 1979.

Gellhorn, E., Kiely, W.F. "Mystical states of consciousness: neurophysiological and clinical aspects." J Nerv Ment Dis. 1972;154:399-405.

Gilbert SL, Dobyns WB, Lahn BT (2005) Genetic links between brain development and brain evolution. Nat Rev Genet 6.

Gray JA. The Psychology of Fear and Stress. 2nd ed. New York, NY: Cambridge University Press; 1988.

Gloor, P. (1992), 'Amygdala and temporal lobe epilepsy', in The Amygdala: Neurobiological Aspects of Emotion, Memory and Mental Dysfunction, ed J.P. Aggleton (New York: Wiley-Liss).

Greenspan, S. I. and S. G. Shanker (2004). The first idea: How symbols, language, and intelligence evolved from our early primate ancestors to modern humans. Cambridge, MA: Da Capo Press.

Grady, D. (1993), 'The vision thing: Mainly in the brain', Discover, June.

Gallagher HL, Frith CD (2003) Functional imaging of 'theory of mind'. Trends Cogn Sci 7: 77.

Gallese V, Fogassi L, Fadiga L, Rizzolatti G (2002) Action representation and the inferior parietal lobule. In: Prinz W, Hommel B (eds) Attention & Performance XIX. Common mechanisms in perception and action. Oxford University Press, Oxford.

Gallese V, Keysers C, Rizzolatti G (2004) A unifying view of the basis of social cognition. Trends Cogn Sci 8: 396–403.

Gangitano M, Mottaghy FM, Pascual-Leone A (2001) Phase specific modulation of cortical motor output during movement observation. NeuroReport 12: 1489–1492.

Gangitano M, Mottaghy FM, Pascual-Leone A (2004) Modulation of premotor mirror neuron activity during observation of unpredictable grasping movements. Eur J Neurosci 20: 2193– 2202.

Goldman AI, Sripada CS (2004) Simulationist models of face-based emotion recognition. Cognition 94: 193–213.

Grèzes J, Costes N, Decety J (1998) Top-down effect of strategy on the perception of human biological motion: a PET investigation. Cogn Neuropsychol 15: 553–582.

Grèzes J, Armony JL, Rowe J, Passingham RE (2003) Activations related to "mirror" and "canonical" neurones in the human brain: an fMRI study. Neuroimage 18: 928–937.

Gross CG, Rocha-Miranda CE, Bender DB (1972) Visual properties of neurons in the inferotemporal cortex of the macaque. J Neurophysiol 35: 96–111.

Hari R, Forss N, Avikainen S, Kirveskari S, Salenius S, Rizzolatti G (1998) Activation of human primary motor cortex during action observation: a neuromagnetic study.

Proc. Natl Acad Sci USA 95: 15061–15065.

Hardy, G. H. (1940). Ramanujan. Cambridge: Cambridge University Press.

Hall, Daniel, Keith Meador, and Harold Koenig. "Measuring Religiousness in Health Research: Review and Critique." Journal of Religion and Health 47, no. 2 (2008)

Harris, Sam, Jonas Kaplan, Ashley Curiel, Susan Bookheimer, Marco Iacoboni, and Mark Cohen. "The Neural Correlates of Religious and Nonreligious Belief." PLoS One 4, no. 10 (October 1, 2009)

Halgren, E. (1992), 'Emotional neurophysiology of the amygdala within the context of human cognition', in The Amygdala: Neurobiological Aspects of Emotion, Memory and Mental Dysfunction, ed J.P. Aggleton (New York: Wiley-Liss).

Halligan PW, Fink GR, Marshal JC, Vallar G. 2003. Spatial cognition: evidence from visual neglect. Trends Cogn Sci.

Handbook of Emotions, Edited by Michael Lewis, Jeannette M. Haviland-Jones, and Lisa Feldman Barrett, The Guilford Press; 3rd edition (2010).

Haggard, P., Clark, S. and Kalogeras,]. (2002) Voluntary action and conscious awareness, Nature Neuroscience 5, 382-5. Haggard, P., Newman, C. and Magno, E. (1999) On the perceived time of voluntary actions. British Journal of Psychology 90, 291-303.

Hameroff, S.R. and Penrose, R. (1996) Conscious events as orchestrated space-time selections. Journal of Consciousness Studies 3(1), 36-53; also reprinted in J. Shear (ed.) (1997) Explaining Consciousness-The Hard Problem. Cambridge, MA, MIT Press, 177-95.

Hardcastle, V.G. (2000) How to understand theN in NCC. InT. Metzinger (ed.) Neural Correlates of Consciousness. Cambridge, MA, MIT Press, 259-64.

Harding, D.E. (1961) On Having no Head: Zen and the Re-Discovery of the Obvious. London, Buddhist Society.

Hardy, A. (1979) The Spiritual Nature of Man: A Study of Contemporary Religious Experience. Oxford, Clarendon Press.

Hamad, S. (1990) The symbol grounding problem. Physica D 42, 335-46.

Hamad, S. (2001) No easy way out. The Sciences 41(2), 36-42.

Harre, R. and Gillett, G. (1994) The Discursive Mind. Thousand Oaks, CA, Sage.

Haugeland, J. (ed.) (1997) Mind Design II: Philosophy, Psychology, Artificial

Intelligence. Cambridge, MA, MIT Press.

Hauser, M.D. (2000) Wild Minds: What Animals Really Think. New York, Henry Holt and Co.; London, Penguin.

Hearne, K. (1990) The Dream Machine. Northants, Aquarian.

Hebb, D.O. (1949) The Organization of Behavior. New York, Wiley.

Helmholtz, H.L.F. von (1856-67) Treatise on Physiological Optics.

Hess, EH (1975) "The role of pupil size in communication," Scientific American, 233(5), 110–12.

Heyes, C.M. (1998) Theory of mind in nonhuman primates. Behavioral and Brain Sciences 21, 101-48; with commentaries.

Heyes, C.M. and Galef, B.G. (eds) (1996) Social Learning in Animals: The Roots of Culture. San Diego, CA, Academic Press.

Hilgard, E.R. (1986) Divided Consciousness: Multiple Controls in Human Thought and Action. New York, Wiley.

Hocquette JF (2016) Is in vitro meat the

solution for the future? Meat Science 120:

167–176

Hodgson, R. (1891) A case of double consciousness. Proceedings of the Society for Psychical Research 7, 221-58.

Hofstadter, D.R. (1979) Code!, Escher, Bach: An Eternal Golden Braid. London, Penguin.

Hofstadter, D.R. and Dennett, D.C. (eds) (1981) The Mind's I: Fantasies and Reflections on Self and Soul. London, Penguin.

Holland, J. (ed.) (2001) Ecstasy: The Complete Guide: A Comprehensive Look at the Risks and Benefits of

MDMA. Rochester, VT, Park Street Press.

Holmes, D.S. (1987) The influence of meditation versus rest on physiological arousal. In M. West (ed.) The Psychology of Meditation. Oxford, Clarendon Press, 81-103.

Holt, J. (1999) Blindsight in debates about qualia. Journal of Consciousness Studies 6(5), 54-71.

Horgan, J. (1994), 'Can science explain consciousness?', Scientific American, 271.

Holloway RL (1996) Evolution of the human brain. In: Lock A, Peters CR (eds) Handbook of human symbolic evolution. Oxford University Press, Oxford

Iacoboni M, Woods RP, Brass M, Bekkering H, Mazziotta JC, Rizzolatti G (1999) Cortical mechanisms of human imitation. Science 286: 2526–2528.

Iacoboni M, Koski LM, Brass M, Bekkering H, Woods RP, Dubeau MC, Mazziotta JC, Rizzolatti G (2001) Reafferent copies of imitated actions in the right superior temporal cortex. Proc Natl Acad Sci USA 98: 13995–13999.

Jeannerod M (1988) The neural and behavioural organization of goal-directed movements. Clarendon Press, Oxford.

Johnson-Frey SH, Maloof FR, Newman-Norlund R, Farrer C, Inati S, Grafton ST (2003) Actions or hand-objects interactions? Human inferior frontal cortex and action observation. Neuron 39: 1053–1058.

Jackson, F. (1982) Epiphenomenal qualia. Philosophical Quarterly 32, 127-36.

James, W. (1890) The Principles of Psychology (2 volumes). London, Macmillan.

James, W. (1902) The Varieties of Religious Experience: A Study in Human Nature. New York and London, Longmans, Green and Co.

Jansen, K. (2001) Ketamine: Dreams and Realities. Sarasota, FL, Multidisciplinary Association for Psychedelic Studies.

Jay, M. (ed.) (1999) Artificial Paradises: A Drugs Reader. London, Penguin.

Jaynes, J. (1976) The Origin of Consciousness in the Breakdown of the Bicameral Mind. New York, Houghton Mifflin.

Johnson, M.K. and Raye, C.L. (1981) Reality monitoring. Psychological Review 88, 67-85.

Kadim I, Mahgoub O, Baqir S et al. (2015) Cultured meat from muscle stem cells: a review of challenges and prospects. J Integr Agr 14: 222–233

Koski L, Iacoboni M, Dubeau MC, Woods RP, Mazziotta JC (2003) Modulation of cortical activity during different imitative behaviors. J Neurophysiol 89: 460–471.

Krolak-Salmon P, Henaff MA, Isnard J, Tallon-Baudry C, Guenot M, Vighetto A, Bertrand O, Mauguiere F (2003) An attention modulated response to disgust in human ventral anterior insula. Ann Neurol 53: 446–453.

Kandel, E. R. In Search of Memory: The Emergence of a New Science of Mind, W. W. Norton & Company (2007).

Kandel E. R. Schwartz JH, Jessel TM. Principles of neural sciences. New York; McGraw Hill, 2000.

Kanizsa, G. (1979), Organization In Vision (New York: Praeger).

Kaloupek DG, Scott JR, Khatami V. Assessment of coping strategies associated with syncope in blood donors. J Psychosom Res. 1985;29:207-214.

Kanwisher, N. (2001) Neural events and perceptual awareness. Cognition 79, 89-113; also reprinted inS. Dehaene (ed.) The Cognitive Neuroscience of Consciousness. Cambridge, MA, MIT Press, 89-113.

Kapleau, Roshi P. (1980) The Three Pillars of Zen: Teaching, Practice, and Enlightenment (revised edn). New York, Doubleday.

Karn, K. and Hayhoe, M. (2000) Memory representations guide targeting eye movements in a natural task. Visual Cognition 7, 673-703.

Kasamatsu, A. and Hirai, T. (1966) An electroencephalographic study on the Zen meditation (zazen). Folia Psychiatrica et Neurologica Japonica 20, 315-36.

Kaiserman-Abramof, I. R., Graybiel, A. M., & Nauta, W. J. (1980). The thalamic projection to cortical area 17 in a congenitally anophthalmic mouse strain. Neuroscience, 5, 41–52.

Kanold, P. O., Kara, P., Reid, R. C., & Shatz, C. J. (2003). Role of subplate neurons in functional maturation of visual cortical columns. Science, 301, 521–525.

Kennedy, H., & Dehay, C. (1988). Functional implications of the anatomical organization of the callosal projections of visual areas V1 and V2 in the macaque monkey. Behav. Brain Res., 29, 225–236.

Kentridge, R.W. and Heywood, C.A. (1999) The status of blindsight. Journal of Consciousness Studies 6(5), 3-11.

Kihlstrom, J.F. (1996) Perception without awareness of what is perceived, learning without awareness of what is learned. In M. Velmans (ed.) The Science of Consciousness. London, Routledge, 23-46.

Kollerstrom, N. (1999) The path of Halley's comet, and Newton's late apprehension of the law of gravity. Annals of Science 56, 331-56.

Kosslyn, S.M. (1980) Image and Mind. Cambridge, MA, Harvard University Press.

Kosslyn, S.M. (1988) Aspects of a cognitive neuroscience of mental imagery. Science 240, 1621-6.

Kinsbourne, M. (1995), 'The intralaminar thalamic nucleii', Consciousness and Cognition, 4.

Kjaer, Troels, Camilla Bertelsen, Paola Piccini, David Brooks, Jorgen Alving, and Hans Lou. "Increased Dopamine Tone during Meditation- Induced Change of Consciousness." Cognitive Brain Research 13, no. 2 (April 2002)

Kölmel HW. 1985. Complex visual hallucinations in the hemianopic field. J Neurol Neurosurg Psychiatry.

Koenig, Harold. "Research on Religion, Spirituality, and Mental Health: A Review." Canadian Journal of Psychiatry 54, no. 5 (May 2009)

Koenig, Harold, ed. Handbook of Religion and Mental Health. San Diego, CA: Academic Press, 1998

Kraepelin E. Psychiatry: A Textbook for Students and Physicians. New York, NY: Science History Publications; 1990.

Lauglin, Charles, John McManus, and Eugene d'Aquili. Brain, Symbol, and Experience. 2nd ed. New York: Columbia University Press, 1992

Lakoff, G. and M. Johnson (1999). Philosophy in the flesh. Basic Books: New York.

LeDoux, J. E. (1996). The emotional brain. New York: Simon & Schuster.

LeDoux, J.E. (1992), 'Emotion and the amygdala', in The Amygdala:

Neurobiological Aspects of Emo- tion, Memory and Mental Dysfunction, ed J.P. Aggleton (New York: Wiley-Liss).

Levin, D.T. and Simons, D.J. (1997) Failure to detect changes to attended objects in motion pictures. Psychonomic Bulletin and Review 4, 501-6.

Levine,J. (1983) Materialism and qualia: the explanatory gap. Pacific Philosophical Quarterly 64, 354-61.

Levine,J. (2001) Purple Haze: The Puzzle of Consciousness. New York, Oxford University Press. Levine, S. (1979) A Gradual Awakening. New York, Doubleday.

Levinson, B.W. (1965) States of awareness during general anaesthesia. British Journal of Anaesthesia 37, 544-6.

Lewicki, P., Czyzewska, M. and Hoffman, H. (1987) Unconscious acquisition of complex procedural knowledge. Journal of Experimental Psychology: Learning, Memory and Cognition 13, 523-30.

Lewicki, P., Hill, T. and Bizot, E. (1988) Acquisition of procedural knowledge about a pattern of stimuli that cannot be articulated. Cognitive Psychology 20, 24-37.

Lewicki, P., Hill, T. and Czyzewska, M. (1992) Nonconscious acquisition of information. American Psychologist 47, 796-801.

Manthey S, Schubotz RI, von Cramon DY (2003). Premotor cortex in observing erroneous action: an fMRI study. Brain Res Cogn Brain Res 15: 296–307.

Mesulam MM, Mufson EJ (1982) Insula of the old world monkey. III: Efferent cortical output and comments on function. J Comp Neurol 212: 38–52.

Naskar, Abhijit. "Homo: A Brief History of Consciousness", 2015

Naskar, Abhijit. "What is Mind?", 2016

Naskar, Abhijit. "Love, God & Neurons: Memoir of A Scientist who found himself by getting lost", 2016

Naskar, Abhijit. "Principia Humanitas", 2017

Naskar, Abhijit. "We Are All Black: A Treatise on Racism", 2017

Naskar, Abhijit. "Either Civilized or Phobic: A Treatise on Homosexuality", 2017

Naskar, Abhijit. "I Am The Thread: My Mission", 2017

Naskar, Abhijit. "The Bengal Tigress: A Treatise on Gender Equality", 2017

Naskar, Abhijit. "Morality Absolute", 2017

Naskar, Abhijit. "Build Bridges not Walls: In the name of Americana", 2018

Naskar, Abhijit. "Fabric of Humanity", 2018

Naskar, Abhijit. "Lives To Serve Before I Sleep", 2019

Naskar, Abhijit. "Citizens of Peace: Beyond the Savagery of Sovereignty", 2019

Naskar, Abhijit. "The Constitution of The United Peoples of Earth", 2019

Naskar, Abhijit. "Neurons Giveth, Neurons Taketh Away | Abhijit Naskar | TEDxIIMRanchi", 2019 https://www.youtube.com/watch?v=BNX-Q0ySm80

Naskar, Abhijit. "Mission Reality", 2019

Naskar, Abhijit. "Operation Justice: To Make A Society That Needs No Law", 2019

Naskar, Abhijit. "Every Generation Needs Caretakers: The Gospel of Patriotism", 2020

Naskar, Abhijit. "Revolution Indomable", 2020

Naskar, Abhijit. "Servitude is Sanctitude", 2020

Naskar, Abhijit. "Good Scientist: When Science and Service Combine", 2020

Newberg, Andrew, and Jeremy Iversen. "The Neural Basis of the Complex Mental Task of Meditation: Neurotransmitter and Neurochemical Considerations." Medical Hypotheses 61, no. 2 (2003).

Newberg, Andrew. "How God Changes Your Brain: An Introduction to Jewish Neurotheology", CCAR Journal: The Reform Jewish Quarterly, Winter 2016.

Newberg, Andrew, and Stephanie Newberg. "A Neuropsychological Perspective on Spiritual Development." In Handbook of Spiritual Development in Childhood and Adolescence, edited by Eugene

Roehlkepartain, Pamela King, Linda Wagener, and Peter Benson. London: Sage Publications, Inc., 2005

Newberg, Andrew. "The Neurotheology Link An Intersection Between Spirituality and Health", Alternative and Complimentary Therapies, Vol 21 No 1, February 2015.

Newberg, Andrew, Nancy Wintering, Dharma Khalsa, Hannah Roggenkamp, and Mark Waldman. "Meditation Effects on Cognitive Function and Cerebral Blood Flow in Subjects with Memory Loss: A Preliminary Study." Journal of Alzheimer's Disease 20, no. 2 (2010)

Nash, M. (1995), 'Glimpses of the mind', Time.

Nesse RM. Proximate and evolutionary studies of anxiety, stress and depression: synergy at the interface. Neurosci Biobehav Rev. 1999;23:895-903.

Nicolelis, Miguel. (2011) "Beyond Boundaries: The New Neuroscience of Connecting Brains with Machines---and How It Will Change Our Lives", Times Books

O'Hara, K. and Scutt, T. (1996) There is no hard problem of consciousness. Journal of Consciousness Studies 3(4), 290-302, reprinted in J. Shear (ed.) (1997) Explaining Consciousness. Cambridge, MA, MIT Press, 69-82.

O'Regan, J.K. (1992) Solving the "real" mysteries of visual perception: the world as an outside memory. Canadian Journal of Psychology 46, 461-88.

O'Regan, J.K. and Noe, A. (2001) A sensorimotor account of vision and visual consciousness. Behavioral and Brain Sciences 24(5), 883-917.

O'Regan, J.K., Rensink, R.A. and Clark,].]. (1999) Change-blindness as a result of "mudsplashes." Nature 398, 34.

Ornstein, R.E. (1977) The Psychology of Consciousness (2nd edn). New York, Harcourt.

Ornstein, R.E. (1986) The Psychology of Consciousness (3rd edn). New York, Pehguin.

Ornstein, R.E. (1992) The Evolution of Consciousness. New York, Touchstone.

Penfield W, Faulk ME (1955) The insula: further observations on its function. Brain 78: 445– 470.

Penrose, R. (1994), Shadows of the Mind (Oxford: Oxford University Press).

Penrose, R. (1989), The Emperor's New Mind: Concerning Computers, Minds and The Laws of Physics (Oxford: Oxford University Press).

Persinger, "'I would kill in God's name' role of sex, weekly church attendance, report of a religious experience and limbic lability" Perceptual and Motor Skills 1997.

Persinger "Experimental simulation of the God experience" Neurotheology 2003.

Persinger, M. A. (1993b). Personality changes following brain injury as a grief response to the loss of sense of self: Phenomenological themes as indices of local lability and neurocognitive restructuring as psycho- therapy. Psychological Reports, 72

Persinger, Corradini, Clement, Keaney, et al "Neurotheology and its convergence with neuroquantology" NeuroQuantology 2010.

Persinger, Koren and St-Pierre "The electromagnetic induction of mystical and altered states within the laboratory" Journal of Consciousness Exploration and Research 2010.

Persinger "Case report: A prototypical spontaneous 'sensed presence' of a sentient being and concomitant electroencephalographic activity in the clinical laboratory" Neurocase 2008.

Persinger and Saroka "Potential production of Hughlings Jackson's "parasitic consciousness" by physiologically-patterned weak transcerebral magnetic fields: QEEG and source localization" Epilepsy & Behavior 28 (2013).

Persinger. "The neuropsychiatry of paranormal experiences". J Neuropsychiatry Clin Neurosci 2001.

Persinger. "Neuropsychological bases of god beliefs", New York: Praeger, 1987

Persinger. "Temporal lobe epileptic signs and correlative behaviors displayed by normal populations", Journal of General Psychology, 1986

Perry BD, Pollard R. Homeostasis, stress, trauma, and adaptation. A neurodevelopmental view of childhood trauma. Child Adolesc Psychiatr Clin N Am. 1998;7:33.

Paré, D. & Llinás, R. (1995), 'Conscious and preconscious processes as seen from the standpoint of sleep-waking cycle neurophysiology', Neuropsychologia, 33.

P. S. de Laplace. Essai Philosophique sur les Probabilites [1814], in Academy des Sciences, Oeuvres Complotes de Laplace, Vol. 7, Gauthier-Villars, Paris (1886).

Perrett DI, Harries MH, Bevan R, Thomas S, Benson PJ, Mistlin AJ, Chitty AJ, Hietanen JK, Ortega JE (1989) Frameworks of analysis for the neural representation of animate objects and actions. J Exp Bio 146: 87–113.

Phillips ML, Young AW, Senior C, Brammer M, Andrew C, Calder AJ, Bullmore ET, Perrett DI, Rowland D, Williams SC, Gray JA, David AS (1997) A specific neural substrate for perceiving facial expressions of disgust. Nature 389: 495–498.

Phillips ML, Young AW, Scott SK, Calder AJ, Andrew C, Giampietro V, Williams SC, Bullmore ET, Brammer M, Gray JA (1998) Neural responses to facial and vocal expressions of fear and disgust. Proc R Soc Lond B Biol Sci 265: 1809–1817.

Puce A, Perrett D (2003) Electrophysiological and brain imaging of biological motion. Philosoph Trans Royal Soc Lond, Series B, 358: 435–445.

Ramachandran VS. Behavioral and magnetoencephalographic correlates of plasticity in the adult human brain. Proc Natl Acad Sci USA 1993; 90: 10413–20.

Ramachandran VS. Phantom limbs, neglect syndromes, repressed memories, and Freudian psychology. Int Rev Neurobiol 1994; 37: 291–333.

Ramachandran VS. Plasticity and functional recovery in neurology. Clin Med 2005; 5: 368–73.

Ramachandran VS, Hirstein W. The perception of phantom limbs. The D. O. Hebb lecture. Brain 1998; 121: 1603–30.

Ramachandran VS, Rogers-Ramachandran D, Cobb S. Touching the phantom limb. Nature 1995; 377: 489–90.

Ramachandran VS, Rogers-Ramachandran D. Phantom limbs and neural plasticity. Arch Neurol 2000; 57: 317–20.

Ramachandran VS, Rogers-Ramachandran D. It's all done with mirrors. Sci Am Mind 2007; 18: 16–9.

Ramachandran VS, Rogers-Ramachandran D. Sensations referred to a patient's phantom arm from another subjects intact arm: perceptual correlates of mirror neurons. Med Hypotheses 2008; 70: 1233–4.

Ramachandran VS, Rogers-Ramachandran D, Stewart M. Perceptual correlates of massive cortical reorganization. Science 1992; 258: 1159–60.

Rizzolatti G, Craighero L (2004) The mirror-neuron system. Annu Rev Neurosci 27: 169–192.

Rizzolatti G, Fogassi L, Gallese V (2001) Neurophysiological mechanisms underlying the understanding and imitation of action. Nature Rev Neurosci 2:661–670.

Rock I, Victor J. Vision and touch: an experimentally created conflict between the two senses. Science 1964; 143: 594–6.

Rose'n B, Lundborg G. Training with a mirror in rehabilitation of the hand. Scand J Plast Reconstr Surg Hand Surg 2005; 39: 104–8.

Royet JP, Plailly J, Delon-Martin C, Kareken DA, Segebarth C (2003) fMRI of emotional responses to odors: influence of hedonic valence and judgment, handedness, and gender. Neuroimage 20: 713–728.

Rozin R Haidt J and McCauley CR (2000) Disgust. In: Lewis M, Haviland-Jones JM (eds) Handbook of Emotion. 2nd Edition. Guilford Press, New York, pp 637–653.

Saxe R, Carey S, Kanwisher N (2004) Understanding other minds: linking developmental psychology and functional neuroimaging. Annu Rev Psychol 55: 87–124.

S. J. Russell and P. Norvig, Artificial intelligence: a modern approach (3rd edition): Prentice Hall, 2009.

Schienle A, Stark R, Walter B, Blecker C, Ott U, Kirsch P, Sammer G, Vaitl D (2002) The insula is not specifically involved in disgust processing: an fMRI study. Neuroreport 13: 2023–2026.

Showers MJC, Lauer EW (1961) Somatovisceral motor patterns in the insula. J Comp Neurol 117: 107–115.

Singer T, Seymour B, O'Doherty J, Kaube H, Dolan RJ, Frith CD (2004) Empathy for pain involves the affective but not the sensory components of pain. Science 303: 1157–1162.

Smith A (1759) The theory of moral sentiments (ed. 1976). Clarendon Press, Oxford.

S. N. Bose (1924). "Plancks Gesetz und Lichtquantenhypothese". Zeitschrift für Physik. 26 (1): 178–181.

Sprengelmeyer R, Rausch M, Eysel UT, Przuntek H (1998) Neural structures associated with recognition of facial expressions of basic emotions Proc R Soc Lond B Biol Sci 265: 1927–1931.

Strafella AP, Paus T (2000) Modulation of cortical excitability during action observation: a transcranial magnetic stimulation study. NeuroReport 11: 2289–2292.

Simonsen R (2015) Eating for the future: veganism and the challenge of in vitro meat. In: Stapleton P, Byers A (Hg). Biopolitics and utopia. Palgrave Macmillan, New York (2015), S 167–190

Tanaka K (1996) Inferotemporal cortex and object vision. Ann Rev Neurosci. 19: 109–140.

Tesla N. "My Inventions", 1919

T. R. Society, "Machine learning: the power and promise of computers that learn by example," ed. The Royal Society, 2017.

Tomasello M, Call J (1997) Primate cognition. Oxford University Press, Oxford.

Tremblay C, Robert M, Pascual-Leone A, Lepore F, Nguyen DK, Carmant L, Bouthillier A, Theoret H (2004) Action observation and execution: intracranial recordings in a human subject. Neurology. 63: 937–938.

Umilta MA, Kohler E, Gallese V, Fogassi L, Fadiga L, Keysers C, Rizzolatti G (2001) "I know what you are doing": a neurophysiological study. Neuron 32: 91–101.

Von Wright G.H., (1963), Norm and Action. A Logical Inquiry, Routledge & Kegan Paul, London.

Von Wright G.H., (1976), "Determinism and the Study of Man", in Essays on Explanation and Understanding, ed. by J. Manninen and R. Tuomela, Reidel, Dordrecht.

Von Wright G.H., (1977), "What is Humanism?", The Lindlay Lecture, University of Arkansas, Lawrence, Kansas.

Von Wright G.H., (1979), "Humanism and the Humanities", in Philosophy and Grammar, ed. by S. Kanger and S. Öhman, Reidel, Dordrecht, pp. 1-16. Reprinted in von Wright (1993).

Von Wright G.H., (1980), Freedom and Determination, North-Holland Publishing Co., Amsterdam.

Von Wright G.H., (1985), Of Human Freedom, The Tanner Lectures on Human Values,

Vol. VI, ed. by S. M. McMurrin, University of Utah Press, Salt Lake City, pp. 107-70. Reprinted in von Wright (1998).

Von Wright G.H., (1993), The Tree of Knowledge and Other Essays, Brill, Leiden.

 Von Wright G.H., (1997), "Progress: Fact and Fiction", in The Idea of Progress, ed. by A. Burgen et al., W. de Gruyter, Berlin, pp. 1-18.

Von Wright G.H., (1998), In the Shadow of Descartes: Essays in the Philosophy of Mind, Kluwer, Dordrecht.

167